YOU STINK AND

THEY KNOW IT!

I0484259

A practical guide to

nailing your next job

interview.

By Danny Johnson

YOU STINK AND THEY KNOW IT!

A practical guide to nailing your next job interview.

You Stink and They Know It! A practical guide to
nailing your next job interview.

Copyright © 2015 by Danny Johnson

All rights reserved. No part of this publication
may be reproduced, distributed, or transmitted in
any form or by any means, without the prior
written permission of the author, except in the
case of brief quotations embodied in critical
reviews and certain other noncommercial uses
permitted by copyright law. For permission
requests, write to the author,
danny@dannyjohnson.com.

Ordering Information:
www.amazon.com

www.dannyjohnson.com

Special discounts are available on bulk purchases
by corporations, associations, and others. For
details, contact the author,
danny@dannyjohnson.com.

Special thanks to Jason Moore for his work on the
book cover/design.

First Edition

ISBN 978-1507715130

To my children: I pray that you follow your dreams. I promise to continue to do everything in my power to help position you for a bright future and teach you principles of love, hard work, and faith. Whether you choose to chase that dream job or run your own business; I am behind you all the way. Thank you for making me proud to be your father everyday.

TABLE OF CONTENTS

Who am I?

My name is Danny Johnson and I have 15 years experience in the corporate world. Throughout my career I have facilitated and/or participated in countless job interviews. The candidates I have interviewed were internal, external, entry-level, and upper management. I have created and edited a variety of interview questions for all levels of employment in many different industries, giving me keen insight into why certain questions are asked and how to answer them. I have the experience and know-how to share with you the secrets to NAILING your next job interview!

I have been exposed to some of the best and worst interview skills and behaviors from all walks of life and all levels of candidacy. I know the feeling of being unemployed. I know the feeling of working hard and going for that internal promotion or chasing that coveted position with an external company and the potential anxiety that comes with it.

Along with my extensive interview experience on both sides of the table, I have years of experience speaking to thousands of people across the United States, analyzing human behavior, and making them laugh. How? I am a comedian. Ha, ha, he's a comedian. No really, I am. I have been performing professionally for 15 years; have won several national contests, appeared on television, and have more than a dozen commercials under my belt. Stand-up comedy was my full-time profession for many years.

During that time I decided to raise a family. I didn't feel the full-time traveling comedian life fit well with raising a family. I gladly went back to the corporate world and now perform on weekends at Comedy Clubs, Corporate or Church events. I was amazed how the skills I gained as a comedian crossed over into the corporate world!

What does comedy have to do with interviewing for a job? EVERYTHING! I captured what I have learned as a Comedian and Corporate Manager and blended it to create the winning tips I've outlined in this book. Among other things, I learned how to use words to my advantage, how to read people, proper tone, and professional etiquette.

Why am I writing this book?

As I gained my experience in interviewing candidates, I noticed a theme; a pattern of behaviors that stood out among potential candidates. Those that I hired displayed certain skills, not on their résumé, that led to them getting hired for the job. I began to apply these best practices in my career and watched as I was able to attain the positions I sought after each and every time. Some of my successful interviews were for internal promotions and some were opportunities outside of the company I was currently employed.

As I progressed in my career I found that friends, family, and peers started to ask me to help them prep for upcoming job interviews. Each individual that came to me had a sense of panic at the very thought of the interview process. I also recognized, what I thought of as obvious interview do's and don'ts, were not so obvious to others. I noticed a very successful track record for those that I coached/mentored. WOW! The simple steps I shared with them, when applied, WORK!

This book is a direct result of me wanting to reach as many people as possible and help you attain that promotion or new job that you desire. I want to take away the anxiety, fear, and worry, on that very important day.

Introduction

You STINK and they know it. Let's face it; we have all been in a situation where we are fortunate enough to have an interview for that promotion or new job opportunity, and are NERVOUS as all get out! Relax, you are not alone. I will share with you the secrets to NAILING your next interview and securing the job of your dreams!

Congratulations! You have a job interview. Whether it's an internal promotion, lateral move to a position that is a better fit, your first job, or an opportunity at a new company; you've booked an interview day and time. Whew! Take a deep breath and relax. This book is designed to prepare you to exceed expectations during that interview in a confident, professional fashion.

I have met too many people that fear the job interview. They get sweaty, stomach cramps, or shake with nervousness at the very thought of having to 'go through' a job interview. I know some people who have avoided them all together, only to complain later in their career that there are no job opportunities! You are going to NAIL that job interview and cease that opportunity!

A quick story...

As I entered the huge lobby to call the next person to interview, I remember thinking how bad we needed to find a candidate to fill this position. It was a new department and we needed a strong leader. I called for Jeff. I received no response from the ten or so candidates sitting in the lobby. I called again, "Jeff please." As I turned to walk back to the conference room, I heard a grumble. I turned to see Jeff rushing towards me taking off his headphones and turning off his phone. He did not hear me call him. His shirt was half untucked and he mumbled something about not knowing how to turn off his cell phone. Before we even sat down Jeff began his interview with a barrage of his credentials and long list of his previous jobs, without giving me a chance for

8

introductions or pleasantries. He continued on and on, even when I attempted to ask the questions I had prepared. The interview lasted 12 minutes.

I remember reviewing Jeff's résumé earlier that morning and looked forward to meeting him. The interview ended, (or the Jeff show as I called it) and I was baffled at the fact that as a result of the interview, I knew absolutely nothing about Jeff, other than his experience. He essentially read me his résumé. It was rare that this candidate gave me a chance to speak or even take notes. He talked nothing of his skills, personal interests, passion for the industry, etc.

His résumé was so promising.

➢ What happened?

➢ What went wrong?

➢ Could this have been avoided?

➢ Is it any wonder that Jeff is looking for a new career?

These are all things we will look at throughout this book.

I want to encourage you to stay positive, think positively, and act with positivity. You will see some mistakes pointed out in this book that you may have made. Don't beat yourself up, I made them as well.

I met a woman I was interviewing in the lobby near the elevators. Her résumé was impressive and I looked forward to meeting her. When I met her she exuded negativity; facial expression, body language, etc. I wondered if she wanted to be there. I asked how she was doing and the response I received was, "Well, I'm here."

Do you think I hired her? BE POSITIVE!

My promise to you...

When you apply these principles, prepare and rehearse your responses, and remain calm and confident; you will NAIL your next job interview!

These simple tips have worked for me, helping me achieve my career goals and secure multiple promotional opportunities!

You will stand out, perhaps get offered a job at a higher pay level than you interviewed for, and secure your financial future!

This book is designed to ensure you blow your competition away in your next job interview! I will walk you through the best practices I have collected and applied and show you how to utilize them in ALL situations during your next job interview. I want to share with you the success

I've had in coaching and mentoring others to secure your dream job!

Early tip

TIP - We haven't even started yet and I feel compelled to share this tip with you already! Experience vs. Strengths. Remember Jeff? He was all too eager to share with me his vast experience. While experience is sometimes important; it is a far cry from your skill set and value you can bring to the company.

I have 30 years of experience playing baseball, but can assure you that I am not going to be the next shortstop for the Yankees! Experience does not always equal job qualification.

WHAT ARE YOUR STRENGTHS? HOW DO THEY RELATE TO THE POSITION YOU ARE APPLYING FOR? HOW HAVE YOU DEMONSTRATED THOSE STRENGTHS IN A RECENT ACHIEVEMENT?

Preparation

Before the Interview

I have a job interview, now what?

Candidate: "What position am I applying for again?"

This is not a good way for an interview to begin, but it did. Without missing a beat, this candidate went on and on about her wonderful sales skills and how she will flourish in this position with her persuasiveness and passion for selling products. She was interviewing for a position on our reporting team, requiring little or no customer interaction or sales, a position she has experience in, per her résumé!

15

Know the position you are interviewing for, know the required/preferred skills, be prepared! Review the job posting in detail and make note of what kind of candidate they are looking to hire. What characteristics does the company value? What function(s) will you be performing in that role? You should know what you are going after and how you plan on describing that to your potential employers in the interview.

Are you prepared?

DAYS/WEEKS leading up to the interview…

You should prepare relentlessly!

At this point you will have received an email or phone confirmation of your interview date/time. If not already known, and the opportunity presents itself, ask who will be interviewing you. Write down those names.

PREPARE!

PREPARE!

PREPARE!

PREPARE!

PREPARE!

Where am I going?

Drive to your interview location, several times if necessary. You should be intimately familiar with where your interview will be located. If the interview is with your current company, walk to the general area so that you know where you are going. Being late to an interview is a BIG no-no. It turns off the interviewer; puts you in a state of panic as you struggle to arrive, and could cause the interview to be cancelled (with no chance of a rescheduled date). If you are late due to no fault of your own, you should have multiple contact numbers to call when you realize you will be late. Your call should be FULL of EMPATHY!

What should I be prepared to bring?

1. Five-seven copies of your résumé on QUALITY stock paper. You would not normally buy this kind of paper; it is worth the investment. Yes, they already have copies of your résumé. BRING MORE! You should always offer the interviewers a copy of your résumé when you sit down at the interview table.

TIP: Your résumé should be professionally written. You should hire a professional or find a trusted friend with a killer résumé to help you.

General tips for your résumé:

➢ Your résumé should be no more than one to two pages.

➢ Your résumé should state clearly how you meet the needs of the position you are looking to secure.

➢ Your résumé should highlight achievements, certifications, projects, etc. with very specific, high-level bullets outlining the 'what and how'. This is not the time to be modest.

➢ Your résumé must be formatted in a way that makes it VERY easy to read.

➢ Triple check for typos.

➢ Eliminate irrelevant information.

➢ Personal affiliations (political, religious, etc.), unless directly related to the company or position you are applying for, can remain off your résumé.

These are some general guidelines for your résumé. I disclose more detail in my one-on-one coaching sessions. Your résumé speaks for you. It is the sales pitch that employers read to determine if you get the interview and more importantly, what questions they are going to ask you in the interview. Your résumé is your highlight reel. A lot of interview questions start with the interviewer scanning your résumé and asking you about certain achievements or experience.

It is safe to say that, at times, your résumé is a general outline of the responses you have prepared for the interview. Take the time to put together a résumé that you are proud of and truly highlights the value you bring to the table.

2. Notepad. New, clean, unwrinkled. This notepad is something the interviewer will look at the entire meeting. It is sitting in front of you as you take notes. It is a pseudo representation of you in the interviewers mind. I recommend a leather (or pleather) binder to house your notepad. (NOTE: Your binder should contain a print out of the email interview confirmation. It has the address and all necessary names/contact information for those interviewing you. No email confirmation?

WRITE IT DOWN!) Sitting in an interview with nothing in front of you looks silly and gives the impression you are unprepared. You will be asked questions that have multiple parts and sub parts. Be prepared to take notes.

3. Pens.

Candidate: "Oh no!" (I look up from taking notes.)

Me: "What is it?"

Candidate: "My pen ran out of ink, I was writing down the question you asked. Do you have a pen I can borrow?"

Me: "No, I do not." (Insert awkward silence)

You should always have a spare. Don't carry around one pen with four words worth of ink in it and have it run out of ink as you explain to me you are someone who is always prepared.

4. Mints. Yes, mints. Not only do they freshen your breath, they help settle your stomach and ease nerves. DO NOT go into the building with a mint in your mouth! NO gum either! DO NOT STRAY from this list!

DO NOT BE THIS PERSON!

Brown bagger: Bringing too much 'luggage' to the interview or unnecessary items is a turn-off. I had a candidate wheel in her laptop, carrying her brown bag lunch; is she moving in?

GIVER: DO NOT bring small gifts for the interviewers. CREEPY.

BRAGGER: DO NOT bring a folder full of your certificates and accomplishments unless the role you are going for requires proof of certification. One candidate I interviewed brought in a folder packed with monthly awards, certificates, and employee of the month pictures; we get it, you're awesome. Use your words to tell me that. I am not sifting through your awards.

What should I be prepared to talk about?

1. You should have a KILLER opening. The most frequently asked question is, "Tell me a little bit about yourself." Your response should be clear, brief, and include both professional and personal highlights. It should be no longer than 45-90 seconds. TOPS!

Example: "Thank you for asking. Personally, I grew up in central Michigan, the oldest of three children in a primarily blue-collar family. I am very close to my family and was the first to earn a college degree, achieving an Associates of Business Management at Michigan State. Shortly after college, growing weary of the cold, I moved to Florida. Most of my career experience is in the sales world, achieving top sales status at a banking

26

call center and local branch bank. I've always had a passion for writing, so I established a mentor relationship with a member of our process development team. I was able to broaden my skill set by recognizing opportunity for improvement and creating new processes within my department. I've written seven new procedures, leading to a 30% increase in overall sales performance. I found this position to be a good opportunity to both leverage my writing skills and provide desirable career growth opportunities."

2. You should have a basic working knowledge of the company or department you are looking to join. A simple internet search of the company can give a brief history of the

company, industry trends, recent high profile stories, etc. Key information to know:

- ➤ Brief company history

- ➤ Recent major transactions

- ➤ Industry trends

- ➤ Recent headlines impacting that field/business

I interviewed with a large bank for a position in their mortgage department and because of my research, was able to engage in some small-talk about mortgage standards and government regulations that hit the headlines recently. It was a great ice-breaker and I landed the position. I had ZERO mortgage experience on my résumé! If you are interviewing for an internal position, make every effort to have some conversation with someone in that department. Do they have a monthly newsletter you normally breeze over because you don't work in that department? Read it! In a perfect world you would have already established a relationship with that department through mentoring or casual socialization. That's a topic for another book.

3. **You should be prepared to talk about YOU!** They are not hiring your résumé, they are hiring you. They are not hiring your experience; they are hiring you and your skills. You should be intricately familiar with YOU. Review the below bullet points and BE THOUROUGHLY PREPARED to discuss the details of the following:

What are your strengths? (Prepare 3-5 to discuss) *See worksheets on pages 98-107

- What are you good at?

- Why?

- How have you applied those skills to a recent situation?

- What are your areas of opportunity? (Weaknesses, although you'll refer to them as 'an area of opportunity') Always avoid negative language.

- Why?

- MOST IMPORTANTLY, what are you doing to develop that area?

NOTE: If answered thoroughly, most interviewers will be satisfied with one 'weakness.'

Example:

Interviewer: "Tell us about your biggest weakness."

Candidate: "One of my greatest strengths is being analytical. I like to analyze a situation and set the appropriate steps in place to exceed expectations on any given project/task. An area of opportunity I've made dramatic progress on is referred to as 'analysis paralysis.' Over-analyzing situations can lead to lack of action. A written project plan helps me create steps and check points to ensure I move forward in a timely fashion without spending unnecessary time on any one given step. This led to increased efficiency and helped me finish my last seven projects ahead of the deadline established by my leadership team."

Notice how I began my answer to the negative question with one of my greatest strengths. I was also specific, showed forward movement, and quantified my results.

What kind of questions are they going to ask me?
Be prepared to answer questions about the following:

- Conflict

- Deadlines

- Working with difficult employees/customers

- Situations in which you had to act without guidance

- Situations in which you didn't agree with management/leadership

- Team-building

- Why are you looking for a new position or why are you looking to leave your current company?

- Morale improvement

- Sales culture

- Problem solving

- Coordinating multiple groups/departments

- Motivation of others/self

- Your career goals

- Forward/innovative thinking

- Big picture thinking

- Leadership

Many of these topics are covered in any one given

response or strength you choose to highlight.

"Did you rehearse the questions that might be asked? Interviews are about content; however, how you answer a question or a scenario is just as important. For example, tell me about your strengths is often easy to answer. Now, how about giving me an example in your career or school when you had to deal with a difficult situation or conflict and how you resolved the issue? You have to recreate the situation and articulate it. Searching for a scenario in your past will create an uncomfortable silence, don't let that happen. Prepare for the interview as if it was a final exam. Many managers will try to get you off of your game or fluster you to see how you react. Your advantage is being prepared; many of your competitors are not."

Mark, Category Director for a large national super-market chain

How am I supposed to answer these questions?

My advice is to look back on your personal and professional life and identify examples for each of these topics. YES, it's a lot of work. It's worth it. There is no substitute for hard work that prepares you for what could be a long, fruitful career.

READ AND APPLY THIS NEXT SENTENCE SEVERAL

TIMES!!!!!!!

Your answers to interview questions should be in a format that shows your method of thinking, how you applied your unique skill set, how you overcame roadblocks, and the end result.

READ THE ABOVE SENTENCE AGAIN UNTIL YOU MEMORIZE

IT!!!!!!!

Let's take a look at a method of responding to interview questions that will make the above statement easy to achieve. You may have heard of this practice before. It may be widely known; but I can assure you, it is rarely used.

What does that mean?

For each answer think:

- What was the situation?

- What was the task at hand?

- What action did I take?

- What was the result?

The *Situation* is what you are asked to do or achieve. Think of your environment, the people involved, the goal set in front of you, and the timeline that was placed before you. Be specific with the exact situation you were put in.

The *Task* is what you identified that needed to be done to accomplish the task or goal put in front of you.

The *Action* is the specific actions you took to accomplish what was placed before you. The interviewer is looking to hear your thought process and the detailed action plan you identified and put into ACTION! Your action plan is the key to your response. It shows your thought process, relationship-building, partnership, and effective use of resources.

The *Result* details the outcome of your executed action plan. Be specific when you quantify your excellent results.

Example:

Interviewer: "Tell me about a time when you had to motivate your team to achieve a goal they did not believe was attainable."

Candidate: "That's a great question, and all too common. I had a team of ten associates and a newly established sales goal of twenty-five units per month for each associate, five more per associate than they had ever achieved. The team was vocal about not being able to achieve that goal. In order to motivate the team to exceed the expectations, I called a team meeting and asked that they help in creating a team action plan for success.

We discussed the following:

- Number of sales needed per day, per associate

- A list of perceived roadblocks to achieving that goal

- A list of best sales practices from each associate

- Ideas of fun games to play during the day to celebrate each sale

- A regular schedule to follow up on our progress

The meeting ended with a clear understanding of our daily goal, the sharing of best practices from each associate, now documented in a central location for all to access when needed, associate ownership of fun sales games to play during the day, and a set in stone follow up schedule to track our progress.

The result was the realization of an achievable daily goal, increased sales skills through best practice sharing, increased accountability, and the now anticipated follow up meeting to share progress. Lastly, it created a sense of team and unity. We ended up hitting 105% of our sales goal and ranked #2 out of 18 sales team in our department!"

SITUATION, TASK, ACTION, RESULT.

NOTE: The interviewer wants to see how you think, how you apply your skills, how it impacts others/the business, your big picture thinking, your demeanor throughout, your relationship building, and the result.

All interview questions are designed to analyze your behavior, application of your skillset, and the result it yielded. You can use personal or professional examples.

"I highly recommend using the STAR method when responding to interview questions. Be concise and include all pertinent details. Be sure to know the purpose of the question and tailor your response accordingly. Include what you've learned and how you've applied it. You can admit mistakes, just be sure to explain how you've fixed them and what you learned from the experience."

Brandon, AVP Property Preservation in a large global bank

Looking for Answers

Think about your current or previous job: what achievements, projects led, tasks, team events, overcoming obstacles, bull dozing roadblocks, motivating others/self, can you reference?

No professional experience? What if you are a single mother? Think of the skill set it takes to balance your schedule with a career, school, and children. What specific actions do you perform every day, week, month to accomplish that? What kind of skill does that require, what steps did you take to get where you are today? What processes did you develop to help you achieve certain tasks?

What if you are currently in a manual labor job and are interviewing for an office position? Did you ever interact with customers, deal with competing deadlines expected of you, and/or create a new process or better way of doing things?

Remember to think of the HOW and not necessarily the WHAT (function) you do. Employers are interested in your passion, know-how, and application of your skills.

Examples of your strengths and how you applied them, your thought process, use of the resources around you, and your relationship building skills can be identified in your personal and professional life.

You can and will find plenty of examples that help you in preparing to NAIL your next job interview.

TIP – In your current role you should be documenting all of your accomplishments, tactics, action plans, successful interactions, etc. This reference tool will help you in the future as you prepare for your next performance review or JOB INTERVIEW! Think of it as a book of your life skills.

See worksheets on pages 98-107.

Reading the non-verbal's

If the interviewer has stopped writing or taking notes, you've either already answered their question (WRAP IT UP), or you are not even in the ball park with your response. In the latter case, don't hesitate to ask a clarifying question to get you back on track.

Watch for interviewers who drift off, look around the room, or appear disinterested. The chances are you have lost them and need to restructure your answer or ask a clarifying question.

Look for frowns, smiles, prolonged eye contact; giving you a good indication of how your response is being received.

If the interviewer has something in between you and them (drink, etc.), and moves it during the interview, this is a non-verbal 'tell', indicating that they are relating to you. Removing barriers of any kind, no matter how small, are often a sign they like you.

If the interviewer mimics your body language, chances are they relate to you and want to connect.

Take the time to read the body language of those you are meeting with and leverage their 'tells' to make a real connection!

Rehearsal

You need to rehearse your interview question responses with a trusted friend. Set some guidelines:

- Tell your friend what your goal is and that this is no time for fooling around

- Dress the part. Literally, role play

- Give your friend a list of some of the interview questions in this book

- Let your friend make up some questions to ask you

- Repeat, repeat, repeat, repeat. You should be able to walk around your house asking yourself interview questions and answering them with clarity, confidence, and fluidity

Who do I select as a partner?

- Not your friend who has been unemployed forever

- Someone with impeccable grammar

- Someone you admire

- Someone who is at the same level or higher than the position you are applying for

- Someone who is willing to give you open and honest feedback

- Someone whose feedback you are open to receiving

- A career or interview coach. An hour long session will do wonders to help you prepare. It's a small investment that goes a long way. I would love the opportunity to coach you one-on-one and be a part of your success story.

www.dannyjohnson.com

Email: danny@dannyjohnson.com

Twitter: @comediandanny

Facebook: Comedian Danny Johnson

www.YouTube.com/comediandanny

The Big Day

The Day of the Interview

You are prepared, you're ready, and your alarm clock goes off the day of the interview, ahhhhhhhhhhhhhhhhh!!!!!!! Relax, take a deep breath.

If your interview is with another company, I suggest you take the day off from your current job. Impromptu meetings, traffic, and other unknowns may put a wrench in your plans to leave. Having the day off lets you set your own schedule, take your time, and raise the level of importance of this significant day. If your interview is internal, do everything you can to block off time around your interview to mentally prepare.

Get up early enough to press your clothes, shower, and get together the items you are bringing to the interview. Eat a balanced meal a few hours before the interview. Take pride in this day, enjoy the day, you are about to NAIL your interview!

Arrive at your destination 30 minutes prior to your interview. Enter the building in time to check-in no more than 15 minutes before your interview.

Those 10-15 minutes before you enter the building are critical. This is your quiet time. Close your eyes, meditate on your hard work, your preparation, today is your day! Have faith! I encourage you to pray. Pray for fluidity of words, confidence, poise, and be thankful for the opportunity to interview for this new career!

Are you wearing that?

I enjoy flip flops as much as the next guy. But please, please dress appropriately.

Men — shirt and tie is a minimum, pressed, clean, and free of holes. No jeans!

Women — business suit or professional looking pants and blouse.

Below is a list of things to avoid. These are things I have seen worn in interviews I facilitated, FOR REAL.

- Giant jewelry: watches, earrings, bracelets, rings. Jewelry is fine, just not rap star caliber bling!

- Low cut shirts. LADIES! We are here to interview you, not them.

- Heels that make you abnormally taller than you are. Please don't make us watch you struggle to walk towards us.

- Shorts, torn clothing, dirty clothing, jeans, FLIP FLOPS!

- Your current company's uniform or shirt.

- Excessive make-up. Apparently, I've interviewed the Joker several times. It's distracting. If you use make-up, use enough to meet your comfort level, not compete in a beauty pageant.

While the list just mentioned may not disqualify you from the opportunity, it doesn't help. You want as many factors working for you as possible. It is a well-known fact that people develop a perception of you within the first ten seconds of meeting you. Make that ten seconds count!

Think about all the times you've met someone for the first time. What perceptions did you make about them based on their appearance, smell, and speech pattern? You automatically made subconscious assumptions about the person you just met based on those characteristics. Think about that when you choose how to show yourself during an interview.

"First impressions really do go a long way. As soon as you step on the property of a potential employer, you should be in interview mode. The person that gives you directions in the parking lot may be a manager or VP at that location. The recruiters could even be watching your arrival from a window. The receptionist is often your first contact when you enter the office. Be extremely polite to that person even if you are lost, late or upset. Bad feedback from the receptionist or admin could cost you the position."

Brooke, Talent Acquisition Manager for a large customer management company

You Stink! (And they know it!)

Literally, you stink. There are very few things worse than having to sit in a room interviewing someone and battling an odor of some kind. Believe me, I am not listening to you, I am trying to identify the smell; pot roast, body odor, mushroom pizza, a combination of all three?

Let me hopefully state the obvious, although from my experience, it is NOT!

- Shower the day of the interview

- Brush your teeth, use mouth wash, mint, etc.

- Use deodorant

- DO NOT work out after you have done the above and then go to the interview!

- Eliminate or severely minimize the use of perfume or cologne. I interviewed a candidate that made my eyes water from the 'splash' of perfume she had on. I left the room for five minutes in the middle of the interview to recover and get some fresh air. I did not hire her.

- DO NOT smoke for a few hours before your interview. I know that is hard for some, but we can smell it. Non-smokers have radar for that smell. Some smokers chain-smoke outside the building before the interview (typically right outside the one-way glass window of the room we are facilitating the interviews, we see you…) and "hide" the smell with perfume or cologne. Assuming most people are non-smokers, it is not only an irritating smell, but creates a

distraction throughout the interview.

Lastly, the perception is always in the back

of the interviewers mind, smokers=smoke

breaks, sometimes more than the allotted

number of breaks. Allow no doubt in the

interviewers mind that you are mindful of

others and a hard-worker.

- NO GUM!

In a room with strangers

Imagine entering a room and introducing yourself to 2-3 strangers who invite you to sit down and explain to them why they should want you to stick around! You are nervous, surprised, intimidated, and just threw up in your mouth. RELAX! If you have followed the principles in this book, you are prepared, confident, and ready to ROCK!

Several things to remember during the interview:

- SMILE! Never underestimate the positive impression you make simply by smiling. Not a creepy, wide, hold it for too long, I got away with something smile. A polite, engaging smile that exudes confidence.

- A firm handshake is appropriate, not a half-shake-half bro-hug, not a limp hand, but firm without hurting them.

- Breathe! Pacing your breath will help you relax and deliver clear answers and keep a steady verbal pace.

- Sit up! When it comes to your posture, think back and up. Shoulders back, chest up, head up. Slouching shows lack of confidence.

- Maintain eye contact without staring. Bounce your eyes from the various interviewers when responding. Reference your notes if necessary.

- Write down an abbreviated version of each question they ask you. It will most likely be a question with multiple parts. Writing it down will help if you need to reference each part of the question, thus ensuring your answer is complete.

- Your responses should be lengthy enough to answer their question (STAR method), but not so lengthy that they stop writing. I've already mentioned this. IT IS WORTH REPEATING! If your interviewers have stopped writing, they either have the answer they are looking for and you are talking too much, or, you are nowhere near the ball park. In the latter case, don't be afraid to ask clarifying questions.

- Stop fidgeting! I know you are nervous. Avoid every urge to tap your pen, wrinkle the corner of your notepad paper, or bounce

your foot up and down.   Remain calm and
breathe.

- Don't be afraid to take a deep breath before
  responding.   This will help calm your nerves
  and come across clear and confident.

- Keep your speech at an even pace, not too
  slow or fast.   Speak clearly and by all
  means, use proper grammar.   Be passionate
  with your responses.   Not infomercial crazy
  passionate, but excited about the
  opportunity.

Now it's your turn

It is imperative that you have questions prepared for the interviewers. 99% of the time they will ask you if you have any questions. Having some key questions for them will let them know you are serious, engaged, and professional. It tells the interviewer you are not just here to interview for a job, but to see if this company/new role is a good fit for you as well. Do NOT talk money. If an offer is to be made, a recruiter will most likely call you to discuss specifics.

You will typically be asked: "What kind of questions do you have for us?"

A great response to this is:

"Thank you for asking. I'm confident I am a good fit for the position. It's important I work for a company that is a good fit for me. I have a few brief questions for you."

Your questions should be brief, clear, and serve a purpose. I recommend having 2-3 questions prepared in advance.

Examples of questions I've used...

"What does success look like?" (Short/long term)

This question is specific to your role. What are you measured on daily, weekly, monthly, etc? This shows the interviewer that you are interested in performing well and want to be in tune with what success looks like.

"Can you describe a typical day for a person in this role?"

This question will give you a good idea of the daily routine you will encounter.

"What is the biggest area of opportunity in this role/department and how do you see this position impacting it in a positive way?"

BAM! You are appealing to the interviewer's pain point(s) and showing them you are interested in helping.

"Describe the current company culture, what are some of things you like about working for this company/department?"

"What are some of the things in place that ensure a healthy work/life balance?"

Family is important to me. I enjoy being home for dinner each night. Asking the above work/life balance question shows the interviewer that you are not just looking for a job, but a healthy career.

There are a host of great questions you can ask. It's important to choose a few that show the following:

- A genuine interest in succeeding

- How you will be measured, a 'day in the life'

- Biggest area of opportunity, long/short term goals

- The need to identify and help any area needing improvement

- A healthy culture/environment and work/life balance

Lastly, I always ask, "Thank you for meeting with me today, I am excited about the opportunity and how I can leverage my skills in this role, what are the next steps in the interview process?"

The answer is typically standard but will give you an idea of the timeframe in which you should follow up. The response is usually, "We have several more people to interview this week and the recruiter will reach out to candidates over the next seven business days."

Phone Interview

What if my interview is over the phone?

The same principles in this book apply even when your interview is over the phone. The most important thing to remember is that they can't see you! Anything that you think you are conveying through facial expressions or body language is out the window. Your tone, clarity, and pace are all the more important!

I recommend you apply the below tips to ensure a successful phone interview:

- Find a well-lit, quiet room where you will not be interrupted. Nothing throws off the rhythm of an interview as a child banging on the door or speaking to you

during the interview. If you have a
dog(s), put them outside!

- Use a land line, or fully charge your cell
  phone in preparation for the interview.
  If your cell phone dies during the
  interview; I can assure you, so do your
  chances of landing that job.

- Use the mute button for coughs, throat
  clearing, etc. Practice these phone
  functions with your friends/family.

- Previously, we discussed role playing the
  interview with a friend/family member. I
  suggest you do the same, over the phone.
  Ask your interview partner for honest
  feedback about how you came across. Were
  you confident, clear, and precise?

- Dress the part. Yes, I know it is a phone interview. Put on an outfit that you would wear to a face-to-face interview. I guarantee if you dress the part, you are more likely to act the part.

- Call in no less than three minutes before your scheduled time. If they are calling you, be prepared ten minutes prior to the interview.

- Have water handy. Dry mouth is clearly heard on the phone and conveys nervousness. Do not eat or chew gum during the phone interview.

- If at all possible, block all incoming calls, sending them to voicemail.

Incoming calls often cause a brief sound block and disrupt the flow of the call.

- At the end of the call, make sure the call is disconnected before speaking freely. I have facilitated phone interviews in which the candidate thought they hung up their cell phone; I heard foul language and improper grammar. DISCONNECT!

- Celebrate! You were spared (at least temporarily) the "dreaded" face-to-face interview. Congratulations!

Start preparing for your face-to-face interview. Once you've nailed the phone interview, then next step is almost always the face-to-face interview. It's important to realize that most likely, the very same people who interviewed you over the phone, will interview you in person. There will most likely be 1-2 additional people that you have never spoken to present during the face-to-face interview.

It is important to reference your notes from the phone interview as you prepare for the in-person interview. You do not want to use all of the same responses. Start preparing new ones and refining the examples you plan on touching upon again. You have the opportunity to blow these people away if your responses in a second or third interview highlight more of your skill and excellence by referencing a new set of examples, different than the phone interview.

Presentation Interview

What if I am asked to participate in a Presentation Interview?

This type of interview is common, particularly for promotional opportunities. I welcome these types of job interviews! Think about it; this gives you a chance to virtually have all of your talking points displayed!

You will receive guidance as to what your presentation should be on or about: how to increase sales numbers, cross-functional coaching opportunities, project management, growth plan, etc.

Confirm the technology requirements. Typically, you are to bring your FULLY CHARGED laptop and accessories.

74

You should NOT read your presentation verbatim! The slides in your presentation are summary bullet points of the presentation you are giving. Think of your presentation as a road map for those watching to follow along as you make your case.

Whatever the topic is, be sure to follow these guidelines:

- Each slide should be professional, clean, uncluttered, have clear points, and be fun to view! You should be able to read your slide in less than 20 seconds. You may talk for longer than 20 seconds about the slide, but your slide should be a concise summary and may even include points you don't touch on.

- Use illustrations where appropriate. I recommend leveraging clip art to help avoid anything proprietary and/or inappropriate.

- Each slide should have the same flow. If slide one has four box's reading left to right, the other slides should be the same or similar.

- Avoid complicated graphs, charts, etc. Keep your slides simple and to the point. Your audience shouldn't have to squint to read your slide.

- Stick to a general outline - Presentation page, Agenda page, Situation, Task, Action/Action items, Result, Summary, and Q & A. Allow time at the end of the interview to answer questions.

- The Agenda page is critical to set the tone, pace, and flow of your presentation. For example, letting the interviewers know there is a Q & A portion of your presentation may help avoid interruptions throughout.

- Print at least five copies of the presentation for the interview. Giving the interviewers a hard copy gives them a sense of permanency that you are confident in the work you created.

- Rehearse this presentation relentlessly. Record it and watch yourself. Include an audience of friends/family. This will also help you time your presentation. Typically, you are instructed as to how much time you have to present.

- Pay particular attention to your body language and posture. Are you slouching? Do you look confident? Do you reference the slides or your notes too often? Analyze your tone, speech pace, and word choice.

- REMEMBER to be specific when outlining your solution. The presentation interview is just another version of them interviewing you. It is important to show your skills, thought process, organizational skills, and ability to lead others. The presentation itself is just an illustration of your talents!

- Show how PASSIONATE you are through the way you deliver your presentation. You are selling yourself! Are you excited about this opportunity?

- Use humor in your slide and/or presentation.
  I had a client, who titled the first page of
  his presentation, 'Project: Hire Tom.' (not
  the printed version of his presentation)
  "Whoops, that's awkward, how did that get
  there?" Everyone in the room got a chuckle
  and it *broke the ice*. He quickly moved to
  slide one and transitioned into his
  presentation. Another one of my clients
  knew the people interviewing him had an
  affinity for a local sports team. He
  inserted the team logo into his first slide.
  My client cleverly tied the success of this
  sports team into his opening, linking it to
  a winning business team and how he can
  contribute. GENIUS!

Post Interview

I recommend a hand-written note mailed to each interviewer. The lost art of a hand-written letter will go a long way. Keep it brief, thanking the interviewers for the opportunity to discuss the position. Mail it immediately after your interview. This typically works well with a smaller company. I've found email to work better with larger companies. If you don't have the interviewers contact information, email the recruiter and ask them to forward your appreciation.

Some companies will contact you before you have a chance to follow-up with them. I once had a company call me to schedule a second interview as I pulled out of the parking lot immediately after finishing my initial interview!

That is a true testament to the principles in this book. APPLY THEM and see!

If you haven't heard from them, place a follow up call 48-72 hours after your interview. Be polite, direct, and clear. Your communication should simply state who you are, who you met with, and that you are excited to hear about the opportunity. You should also let them know that you are willing to meet again if they have any additional questions.

Finally, CELEBRATE! You prepared for and NAILED your job interview! That takes courage and dedication.

Weirdest questions I've been asked as the interviewer

I have seen and heard it all from candidates I've interviewed. I hope you find these amusing and keep them as a mental list of things NEVER to use in an interview.

"So, when do I start?" (Asked of me after the interview ended)

The principles in this book, if applied, should increase your confidence to NAIL the interview. Leave your arrogance at home.

"Where the bathrooms at?"

Handle your business before the interview, or at the very least ask that question using proper grammar.

"I hated my last job."

While that may be true of your last job or last set of co-workers, avoid negative language of any kind. Use words like challenging, obstacle, opportunity for improvement, etc.

"Have your job." (In response to, "What are your long and short term goals?")

Seeking promotional opportunities is a great goal to achieve. Avoid making it personal. What if the interviewer likes his position and wants to stay in it until they retire? Does he have to worry about you plotting for his job?

"Become a nurse." In response to, "What are some of your specific career goals?" (Interviewing for a Customer Service Sales position.)

If your future involves a career outside of the company you are interviewing with, in a totally different field, AVOID sharing that information. Your response should focus on your skill set and career progression in an environment that leverages those talents.

"Man, you ask some tough questions."

YOU ARE GOING TO NAIL THIS JOB INTERVIEW! Stop telling us you are not! If you struggle responding to a particular question you can reply with: "Great question, if I understand you correctly, you are looking for… (Insert a summary of the question)." This will buy you some mental time to gather your response.

Weirdest or most common questions I've ever been asked as the interviewee

I thought it would be valuable to share with you some of the oddest and/or most frequent questions I have heard from interviewers; these will help you in your preparation.

"Why you? We have plenty of candidates, why you?" (Asked of me as the interviewer closed his notebook)

I have since adopted this question when I interview candidates. This question is designed to throw you off. You just spent close to an hour detailing your expertise and value. NOW, they want to know WHY ME? Remain calm and use this time as an opportunity to give your 'elevator speech.' An elevator speech is best described as

85

what you would say to sell yourself if you were in an elevator with the CEO and he/she asked what you would bring to the company. Be clear, confident, and precise when summarizing your value.

"Why are you looking for a new position?", or "Why are you looking to leave your current company?"

Be careful. The interviewer wants to see your motive and to see if you will bad-mouth your current department or company. No one likes a gossip or a negative Nelly. This is a response you should have prepared ahead of time. Your answer should NEVER be for more money or to seek a promotional opportunity. Tie your answer to your skill set, your job responsibilities, and your future.

Example answer: "What intrigued me most about this role was how my sales skills and experience can be leveraged to help promote the growth that this market is experiencing. I am happy in my current role/company, but view this opportunity as one that best utilizes my skills to their fullest potential."

Simple, clear, positive!

"Why would I want to work with you?"

This question is important; the way you answer is even more important. Chances are this is a position in which you will be working directly with the person(s) interviewing you. The interviewer's want to know what it is like working with you for at least eight hours a day for the next few years, or more! Your answer should be professional and positive. Describe how easy it is to work with you, how you like to develop real relationships, have a good sense of humor, and handle conflict with poise.

"Did you have a hard time finding the place?"

This question is designed to gage your preparation for the day and to see how serious you are about this opportunity. "Not at all, I knew exactly where to go, I am very excited to meet with you about this opportunity." NEVER complain about how big the city is, how bad the traffic is, how complicated the campus is, the fact that you couldn't find a parking spot, couldn't see the building numbers, etc. Remain positive and friendly, you are prepared!

What does the internet say about you?

Some employers will search for you online
before hiring you. What will they see on your
social media sites? My advice is to research
yourself before the interview. Make every effort
to delete unwanted content and make all of your
profiles private. This will prevent some wacko
you knew in high school from posting an old
picture of you passed-out wearing a goat costume.

Put your name and city in a search engine and
see what pops up. Audit every one of your social
media accounts and clean them up. Pictures,
profanity, party scenes, etc. When reviewing your
social media accounts, step outside yourself and
ask, "Would I want this person representing my
company in a managerial role I am looking to
fill?"

Take your time when researching yourself online, your potential employer will. Go four, five, six pages deep in the search engine. Ask a trusted friend to search you online to see what they find. You will be surprised.

Lastly, keep your online content in mind going forward; with this new job or promotion, you now represent that company. Social media content and pictures sometimes appear in local newspapers and TV shows, in a bad way. Be mindful of how you put yourself out there and who has access to post content on your accounts.

Conclusion

In this book you've learned interview prep, technique, and execution. Apply these tools with confidence and I assure you that you will land your next dream job!

It should be mentioned there is another benefit of interviewing strong. Interviewing strong may lead to you being hired for a position BETTER than the one you actually interviewed for! I remember interviewing several candidates for sales associate positions, only to offer them a manager role instead. They interviewed with excellence, showed me their unique skill set, leadership, and drive to succeed. The same goes for managerial interviews turning into an Executive hire.

You can do this! I am not suggesting you take a role out of your scope, but certainly be open to the idea of taking a higher level position! A lot of times companies are hiring for a multitude of openings and you may be a qualified candidate for a higher position. It is easier for them to fill the slot with a well-qualified candidate already in their office than setting up a whole new set of interviews!

I look forward to your success stories. Please email me at danny@dannyjohnson.com and share your feedback! I am also available for personal one-on-one coaching, group coaching, workshops, and speaking engagements. I welcome the opportunity to help you secure your dream job!

My coaching extends beyond interview preparation. I will assist you in negotiating the salary and perks you want! I can share with you the time-tested techniques that will garner you the salary and job benefits you want. Employers consider many factors when offering compensation. I will coach you through this process starting with receiving the offer, the research required to determine a counter offer, and exactly how to articulate this to your potential employer. I will also share with you how to network internally and externally to secure that coveted career opportunity. Often times, just getting an interview is a challenge. I will coach you through the steps necessary to expand your network of contacts and build lasting relationships that will nourish your career path. Do you run your own business? Great! I will share with you the sure-fire techniques to hiring and retaining the ideal candidate.

Having the right people in the right role is a key factor to your business's success!

Thank you for taking the time to invest in you. See you at the top!

Testimonials

"Being mentored by Danny Johnson changed my life. I found myself in a position with a great company and my performance was "top notch." I couldn't help but feel that a few promotional opportunities out there better fit my skill set and would provide me with better job satisfaction. I talked to Danny about applying for a new job opportunity. He provided me with résumé and interviewing tips that I leveraged in several interviews. I am happy to report that I landed the position I so much coveted and love it! Talking with Danny and applying the techniques he outlines, kept me encouraged and confident. Thank you Danny for your guidance, rock solid interview techniques, and motivation!"

Kimberly, Consumer Operations Associate

"I found myself in a foreign land as I pursued my most recent promotion. The interview was set to be a presentational interview rather than the typical question/answer style I have facilitated and participated in personally countless times. I struggled to piece together my ideas and form them into a cohesive 30 minute presentation on how I could help the organization be more successful. I reached out to Danny. *Danny is a stand-up guy*! Immediately after requesting some face-time, we setup a meeting and went to work. Danny helped me put my ideas in place and gave me some tips on how to effectively present my ideas. Danny reinforced a variety of interview best practices; such as staying positive, providing clear and concise responses, and most importantly, proper preparation techniques! His advice and direction

helped me secure the promotion. I refer anyone
looking for interview preparation help or
presentation help to Danny Johnson. Thanks again
for your guidance. It helped me gain the
confidence, skills, and tools I need to continue
my success!"

Nick, Assistant Vice President, Sales

Worksheet: Finding your strengths

List accomplishment, life event, project, award, etc.	What action steps did you take to achieve your goal?	What character traits or skills did this take?	Strength discovered
<u>Example:</u> Recognized by manager for sales performance.	Solicited best practices Took extra training courses Connected with customer through listening to their needs	Self-starter Taking initiative Application of learning Self-awareness	Leadership Drive Passionate about self-improvement

Worksheet: Articulating your interview responses

Strength #1 _____

What was the situation in which you applied this strength?

_____

_____

_____

_____

What tasks did you identify that needed to be done?

_____

_____

_____

_____

Describe your action plan, how you overcame roadblocks, leveraged resources, specific action items, etc.

_____

_____

_____

_____

What was the result?

_____

_____

_____

_____

Worksheet

Strength #2 _____

What was the situation in which you applied this strength?

_____

_____

_____

_____

What tasks did you identify that needed to be done?

_____

_____

_____

_____

Describe your action plan, how you overcame roadblocks, leveraged resources, specific action items, etc.

_____

_____

_____

_____

What was the result?

_____

_____

_____

_____

Worksheet

Strength #3 _____

What was the situation in which you applied this strength?

_____

_____

_____

_____

What tasks did you identify that needed to be done?

_____

_____

_____

_____

Describe your action plan, how you overcame roadblocks, leveraged resources, specific action items, etc.

_____

_____

_____

_____

What was the result?

_____

_____

_____

_____

Worksheet

Strength #4 _____

What was the situation in which you applied this strength?

_____

_____

_____

_____

What tasks did you identify that needed to be done?

_____

_____

_____

_____

Describe your action plan, how you overcame roadblocks, leveraged resources, specific action items, etc.

_____

_____

_____

_____

What was the result?

_____

_____

_____

_____

About the Author

For well over a decade Danny Johnson has facilitated countless job interviews, written interview questionnaires, and helped several large U.S. companies build entire departments from scratch; helping them hire the right candidate(s) for the right role(s). Danny is also an accomplished Comedian and Actor; having performed at Comedy Clubs, Corporate Events, and Churches, all over the United States. Danny has starred in over a dozen of commercials, a variety of voice-over spots, won multiple comedy contests, and appeared on Comedy Central's Laugh Riots.

Danny's dual career track allows him to blend his corporate experience, study of human behavior through years of stand-up comedy, and his own personal application of the principles in this book to outline how you will nail your next job interview!

Resources

Danny is available for speaking engagements, workshops, one-on-one coaching, stand-up comedy, acting or voice-over work.

www.dannyjohnson.com

Email: danny@dannyjohnson.com

Twitter: @comediandanny

Facebook: Comedian Danny Johnson

www.YouTube.com/comediandanny

www.ingramcontent.com/pod-product-compliance
Lightning Source LLC
Chambersburg PA
CBHW070817180526
45168CB00002B/645